MANNERS MATTER TO MAEVIS

Maevis IS KIND

Written by
Vicky Bureau
M.S., School Counseling

Illustrated by
Flavia Zuncheddu

A Starfish Book

SEAHORSE
PUBLISHING

Teaching Tips for Caregivers:

As a caregiver, you can help your child succeed in school by giving them a strong foundation in language and literacy skills and a desire to learn to read.

This book helps children grow by letting them practice reading skills.

Reading for pleasure and interest will help your child to develop reading skills and will give your child the opportunity to practice these skills in meaningful ways.

- Encourage your child to read on her own at home
- Encourage your child to practice reading aloud
- Encourage activities that require reading
- Establish a reading time
- Talk with your child
- Give your child writing materials

Teaching Tips for Teachers:

Research shows that one of the best ways for students to learn a new topic is to read about it.

Before Reading

- Read the "Words to Know" and discuss the meaning of each word.
- Read the back cover to see what the book is about.

During Reading

- When a student gets to a word that is unknown, ask them to look at the rest of the sentence to find clues to help with the meaning of the unknown word.
- Ask the student to write down any pages of the book that were confusing to them.

After Reading

- Discuss the main idea of the book.
- Ask students to give one detail that they learned in the book by showing a text dependent answer from the book.

TABLE OF CONTENTS

Meet Maevis

This is Maevis.

School **manners** matter to Maevis.

School manners are the rules and expectations for learning.

Being Kind

One important school manner is being kind.

When Maevis is kind, it means she is thinking about how others feel.

BE
KIND

Being kind is more than just being nice.

Kindness is much deeper.

Ways to Be Kind

Being kind means it makes you happy to make others happy.

Maevis can be kind in many different ways.

Maevis can be **friendly**.

Maevis is kind when she makes a new friend.

Maevis can be **thoughtful**.

Maevis is kind when she makes a card for her teacher when he’s sick.

GET
WELL
SOON

Maevis can be **generous**.

Maevis is kind when she gives her last cookie to her sister.

Sometimes, it's hard for Maevis to be kind.

And there’s not always a **reward** for being kind.

But when Maevis is kind to others...others are kind to Maevis.

And that's the biggest reward of all!

It makes Maevis happy to
make others happy.

And that's why Maevis is kind!

WORDS TO KNOW

friendly (FREND-lee): welcoming, kind, and pleasant toward others

generous (JEN-ur-uhs): willing to give or share; not selfish

manners (MAN-urs): the rules and expectations for learning; good behaviors

reward (ri-WORD): something of value that is promised to someone for good work or good actions

thoughtful (THAWT-fuhl): having or showing careful thought

INDEX

COMPREHENSION QUESTIONS

1. What does it mean to be kind?
2. Based on the story, name one way you can be kind to others.
3. On page 16, how does Maevis show generosity toward others?
4. What reward does Maevis get for being kind to others?

ABOUT THE AUTHOR

Vicky Bureau was born in Longueuil, Quebec, and was raised in South Florida. As a teacher, she developed a passion for the social and emotional growth of her students and later transitioned into the area of child and adolescent psychology after earning her master's degree in school counseling.
In addition to working with children, Vicky loves to be surrounded by animals and nature. She lives in Fort Lauderdale with her family: Billy, Khloe, M.J., and Max; her three cats, Alley, Baguette, and Salem; and her dog, Boomer.

Written by: Vicky Bureau
Illustrated by: Flavia Zuncheddu
Design by: Under the Oaks Media
Editor: Kim Thompson

Library of Congress PCN Data
Maevis Is Kind / Vicky Bureau
Manners Matter to Maevis
ISBN 978-1-63897-463-5(hard cover)
ISBN 978-1-63897-578-6(paperback)
ISBN 978-1-63897-693-6(EPUB)
ISBN 978-1-63897-808-4(eBook)
Library of Congress Control Number: 2022932719

Printed in the United States of America.

Seahorse Publishing Company
www.seahorsepub.com

Published in the United States
Seahorse Publishing
PO Box 771325
Coral Springs, FL 33077

SEAHORSE PUBLISHING